Mercury and Water-Quality Data from Rink Creek, Salmon River, and Good River, Glacier Bay National Park and Preserve, Alaska, November 2009–October 2011

By Sonia A. Nagorski, Edward G. Neal, and Timothy P. Brabets

Prepared in cooperation with the National Park Service

Open-File Report 2013-1097

U.S. Department of the Interior
U.S. Geological Survey

U.S. Department of the Interior
SALLY JEWELL, Secretary

U.S. Geological Survey
Suzette M. Kimball, Acting Director

U.S. Geological Survey, Reston, Virginia: 2013

For more information on the USGS—the Federal source for science about the Earth, its natural and living resources, natural hazards, and the environment, visit http://www.usgs.gov or call 1–888–ASK–USGS.

For an overview of USGS information products, including maps, imagery, and publications, visit http://www.usgs.gov/pubprod

To order this and other USGS information products, visit http://store.usgs.gov

Suggested citation:
Nagorski, S.A., Neal, E.G., and Brabets, T.P., 2013, Mercury and water-quality data from Rink Creek, Salmon River, and Good River, Glacier Bay National Park and Preserve, Alaska, November 2009–October 2011: U.S Geological Survey Open-File Report 2013-1097, 20 p., http://pubs.usgs.gov/ofr/2013/1097.

Contents

Figures

Tables

Tables—Continued

Conversion Factors, Datums, and Abbreviations and Acronyms

Conversion Factors

Multiply	By	To obtain
Length		
centimeter (cm)	0.3937	inch (in.)
millimeter (mm)	0.03937	inch (in.)
meter (m)	3.281	foot (ft)
kilometer (km)	0.6214	mile (mi)
Area		
square kilometer (km^2)	247.1	acre
square kilometer (km^2)	0.3861	square mile (mi^2)
Volume		
liter (L)	1.057	quart (qt)
liter (L)	0.2642	gallon (gal)
Flow rate		
cubic meter per second (m^3/s)	35.31	cubic foot per second (ft^3/s)

Temperature in degrees Celsius (°C) may be converted to degrees Fahrenheit (°F) as follows:

$$°F= (1.8×°C)+32.$$

Concentrations of chemical constituents in water are given either in milligrams per liter (mg/L) or micrograms per liter (µg/L).

Datums

Vertical coordinate information is referenced to the North American Vertical Datum of 1988 (NAVD 88).

Horizontal coordinate information is referenced to the North American Datum of 1983 (NAD 83).

Elevation, as used in this report, refers to distance above the vertical datum.

Conversion Factors, Datums, and Abbreviations and Acronyms—Continued

Abbreviations and Acronyms

Certain measurements used in this report are given only in metric units:

ng/L	nanogram per liter
ng/s	nanogram per second
ng/s/km^2	nanograms per second per square kilometer
ng/g	nanograms per gram
L/mg C * m	liters per milligram carbon times meter
GBNPP	Glacier Bay National Park and Preserve
BMI	benthic macroinvertebrates
BTHg	biota total mercury
DOC	dissolved organic carbon
FMHg	filtered methylmercury
FTHg	filtered total mercury
HCl	hydrochloric acid
Hg	mercury
Hg$_T$	total mercury
MeHg	methylmercury
MDN	Mercury Deposition Network
MRL	Mercury Research Laboratory
NWIS	National Water Information System
PTHg	particulate total mercury
SUVA	specific ultraviolet absorbance
USGS	U.S. Geological Survey
UVA	ultraviolet absorbance

Mercury and Water-Quality Data from Rink Creek, Salmon River, and Good River, Glacier Bay National Park and Preserve, Alaska, November 2009–October 2011

By Sonia A. Nagorski[1], Edward G. Neal[2], and Timothy P. Brabets[2]

Abstract

Glacier Bay National Park and Preserve (GBNPP), Alaska, like many pristine high latitude areas, is exposed to atmospherically deposited contaminants such as mercury (Hg). Although the harmful effects of Hg are well established, information on this contaminant in southeast Alaska is scarce. Here, we assess the level of this contaminant in several aquatic components (water, sediments, and biological tissue) in three adjacent, small streams in GBNPP that drain contrasting landscapes but receive similar atmospheric inputs: Rink Creek, Salmon River, and Good River.

Twenty water samples were collected from 2009 to 2011 and processed and analyzed for total mercury and methylmercury (filtered and particulate), and dissolved organic carbon quantity and quality. Ancillary stream water parameters (discharge, pH, dissolved oxygen, specific conductance, and temperature) were measured at the time of sampling. Major cations, anions, and nutrients were measured four times. In addition, total mercury was analyzed in streambed sediment in 2010 and in juvenile coho salmon and several taxa of benthic macroinvertebrates in the early summer of 2010 and 2011.

Introduction

Mercury (Hg) is a global pollutant, dispersed over broad scales by atmospheric mixing and reaching remote areas where it is neither used nor produced (Nriagu and Pacyna, 1988; Fitzgerald and others, 1998). It is carried to Alaska by long-range atmospheric pathways (Schroeder and Munthe, 1998), and, upon deposition, it may be methylated and biomagnified as it passes up trophic levels (Wiener and others, 2003).

Although Hg emissions in the United States have decreased in recent decades, global emissions continue to increase, particularly in Asia (Pacyna and others, 2010). Specifically, China has been increasing its coal combustion by 12 percent per year since 2000, accounting for 46 percent of the world's use (Bradsher and Barboza, 2006; U.S. Energy Information Administration, 2012). Models show that much of the Hg released as a by-product of this coal combustion is carried atmospherically to the northern Pacific Ocean and northwest coast of North America (Dastoor and Larocque, 2004; Sunderland and others, 2009). Currently (2012), anthropogenic mercury deposition to Alaska appears to be similar in magnitude to that in temperate latitudes although local sources are minimal and scarce (Fitzgerald and others, 2005).

Little is known about Hg contamination in southern Alaska, even though available evidence indicates that the region increasingly is accumulating this toxin from atmospheric deposition or from biovectors from distant sources (Engstrom and Swain, 1997; Day and others, 2006). A National Park Service contaminant survey conducted in the region in 2007 provided an initial evaluation of Hg distribution in water, sediment, macroinvertebrate, and juvenile coho salmon (Nagorski and others, 2011). This project determined that, streams draining older, wetland-rich landscapes generally had higher total Hg and methylmercury (MeHg) concentrations than young, glacier-fed or recently deglaciated streams. The 2007 survey was based on a single-event sampling and, therefore, trends were not examined.

[1]University of Alaska Southeast

[2]U.S. Geological Survey

Purpose and Scope

With this project, we aimed to evaluate the temporal dynamics of Hg in three adjacent streams draining different landscape types—peatland-rich, peatland-forest mixed, and forest or meadow only. The main objectives of this study are to (1) measure Hg concentrations in water, sediment, and biota of three streams in Glacier Bay National Park and Preserve (GBNPP), Alaska, and to assess differences in Hg and MeHg (if any) among the streams, (2) examine the extent of temporal variation in concentrations and fluxes of total Hg and MeHg in the streams over an annual time period, and (3) provide a detailed baseline dataset for three streams in GBNPP to which future contaminant monitoring efforts may be compared.

This report contains water-quality and climate data collected by the U.S. Geological Survey (USGS) and other agencies from November 2009 to October 2011 at three stream sites, one atmospheric deposition site, and one climate station in GBNPP. Because some of the data presently (2012) cannot be stored in the USGS National Water Information System (NWIS), this report provides a single source to disseminate data that might not otherwise be available to the public.

Description of Study Area

The three study watersheds are directly adjacent to one another and located along the southeastern border of GBNPP and the town of Gustavus (fig. 1A). The Good River and about 10 percent of the Salmon River lie within the Gustavus forelands, a broad, low-elevation and low-relief area about 14 km in width (fig. 1B). The forelands are bordered to the west by a northeast-trending terminal moraine, formed about 250 years ago at the culmination of glacial ice advance during the Little Ice Age (Connor and others, 2009). To the east, the Gustavus forelands are flanked by the northwest-trending Excursion Ridge, which has been free of ice cover for about 13,000 years and rises to an elevation of about 1,050 m. Excursion Ridge is composed of upper Silurian rocks of the Alexander terrane—mostly limestones and mudstones of the Tidal Formation—that are covered by thick peat deposits and contain little forest cover (Rossman, 1963). The Gustavus forelands are composed of about 1,000 years of glacial deposits (largely outwash sands and silts) that overlay uplifted shallow marine sediments (Streveler, 1996).

The headwaters of the Good River originate from the terminal moraine, and flow through a mixture of spruce forest, horsetail, and herbaceous wet meadow. The Salmon River, located between Good River and Rink Creek, collects flow from the peatland-rich Excursion Ridge through a major upper tributary, and from the spruce forest and wet meadow zones of the Gustavus forelands. Rink Creek collects most of its flow from Excursion Ridge. Rink Creek is a sandy-bottomed, organic-rich stream typical of many peatland drainages across southeastern Alaska. Peat accumulations in coastal southeastern Alaska commonly are greater than 1 m deep, and this likely is true for Excursion Ridge (Fellman and others, 2007).

Of the three streams, the Salmon River is the largest and is the best supporter of established anadromous fish runs, including coho (*Oncorhynchus kisutch*), chum (*O. keta*), and pink salmon (*O. gorbuscha*) as well as Dolly Varden (*Salvelinus malma malma*) and steelhead trout (*O. mykiss*) (Alaska Department of Fish and Game, 2005). The Good River supports coho and chum salmon, and Rink Creek hosts coho and pink salmon, cutthroat trout, and Dolly Varden. Stream sampling locations, stream lengths, and elevations are provided in table 1.

The percentage of each watershed covered by wetlands varies from 19 percent to 59 percent according to delineations by the National Wetlands Inventory Classification (U.S. Fish and Wildlife, variously dated) (table 2, fig. 2). The wetlands in the Gustavus Forelands, which include all of the Good River wetlands and about 10 percent of the Salmon River wetlands, are much younger with thinner organic matter deposits compared with the thick peatland accumulations that blanket Excursion Ridge in the Rink Creek and Salmon River watersheds.

Climate

The study area has a wet, moderate marine climate owing to frequent weak high-pressure systems in the summer and the dominance of a strong Aleutian Low in the northern Gulf of Alaska in the autumn, winter, and spring. According to records dating back to 1950 from the National Weather Service climate station at Gustavus (National Oceanic Atmospheric Association, variously dated), January is the coldest month, with an average temperature of -4.0 degrees Celsius (°C), and July is the warmest month, with an average temperature of 12.8°C. Average annual temperature is 4.8°C. Mean annual precipitation is 141 cm, and average annual snowfall is 193 cm. The area typically has intermittent snowpack near sea level and continuous snow cover at elevations above 300 m during winter and early spring. Figures 3 and 4 show the daily precipitation and air temperature maxima and minima in Gustavus during the period of sampling.

A.

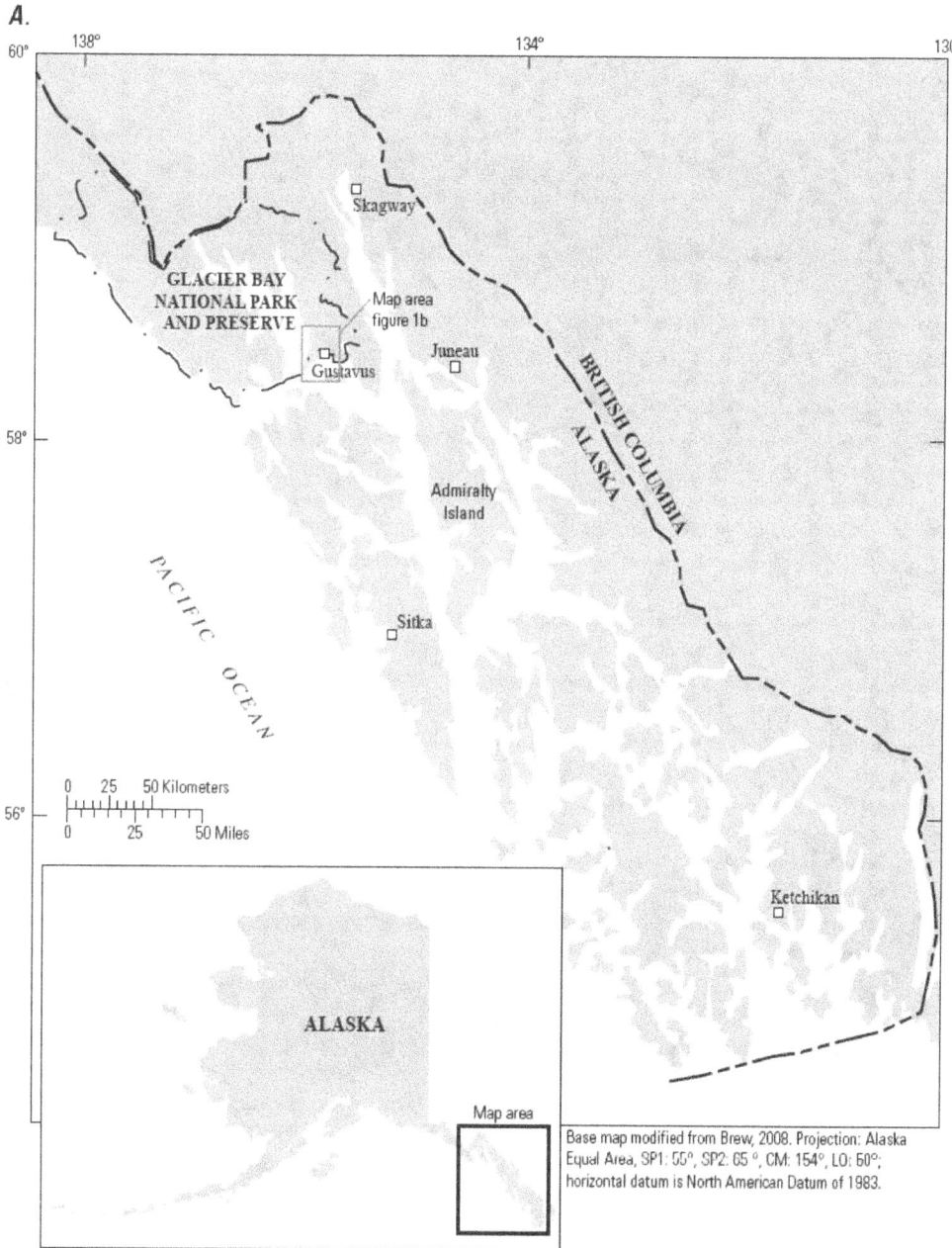

Figure 1.   Locations of (*A*) Glacier Bay National Park and Preserve, and (*B*) aerial image of Rink Creek, Salmon River, and Good River watersheds and sampling sites, Alaska.

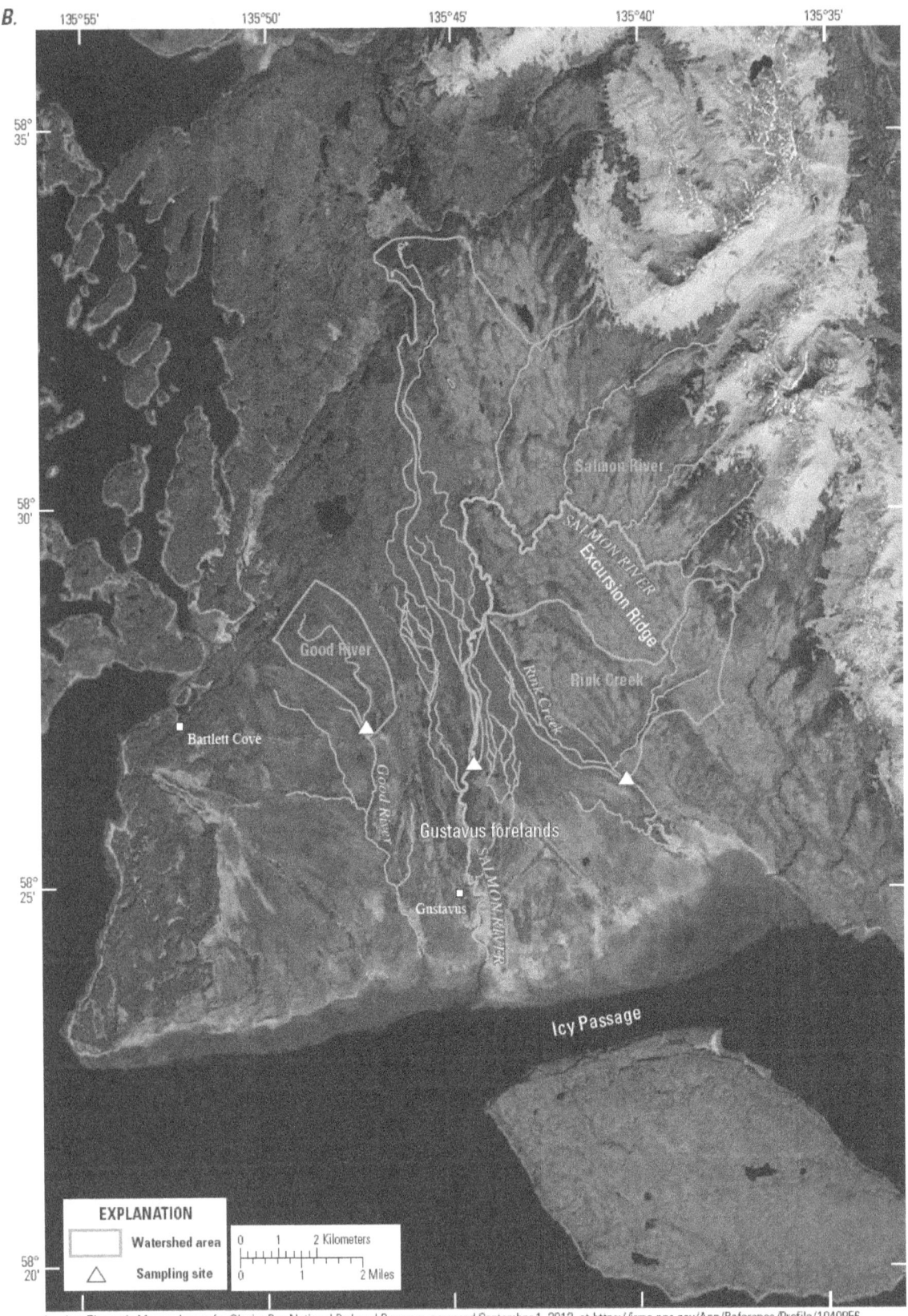

Landsat Thematic Mapper Image for Glacier Bay National Park and Preserve, accessed September 1, 2012, at https://irma.nps.gov/App/Reference/Profile/1040856. Hydrography from National Hydrographic Dataset. Projection: Alaska Equal Area, SP1: 55°, SP2: 65 °, CM: 154°, LO: 50°; horizontal datum is North American Datum

Figure 1.—Continued

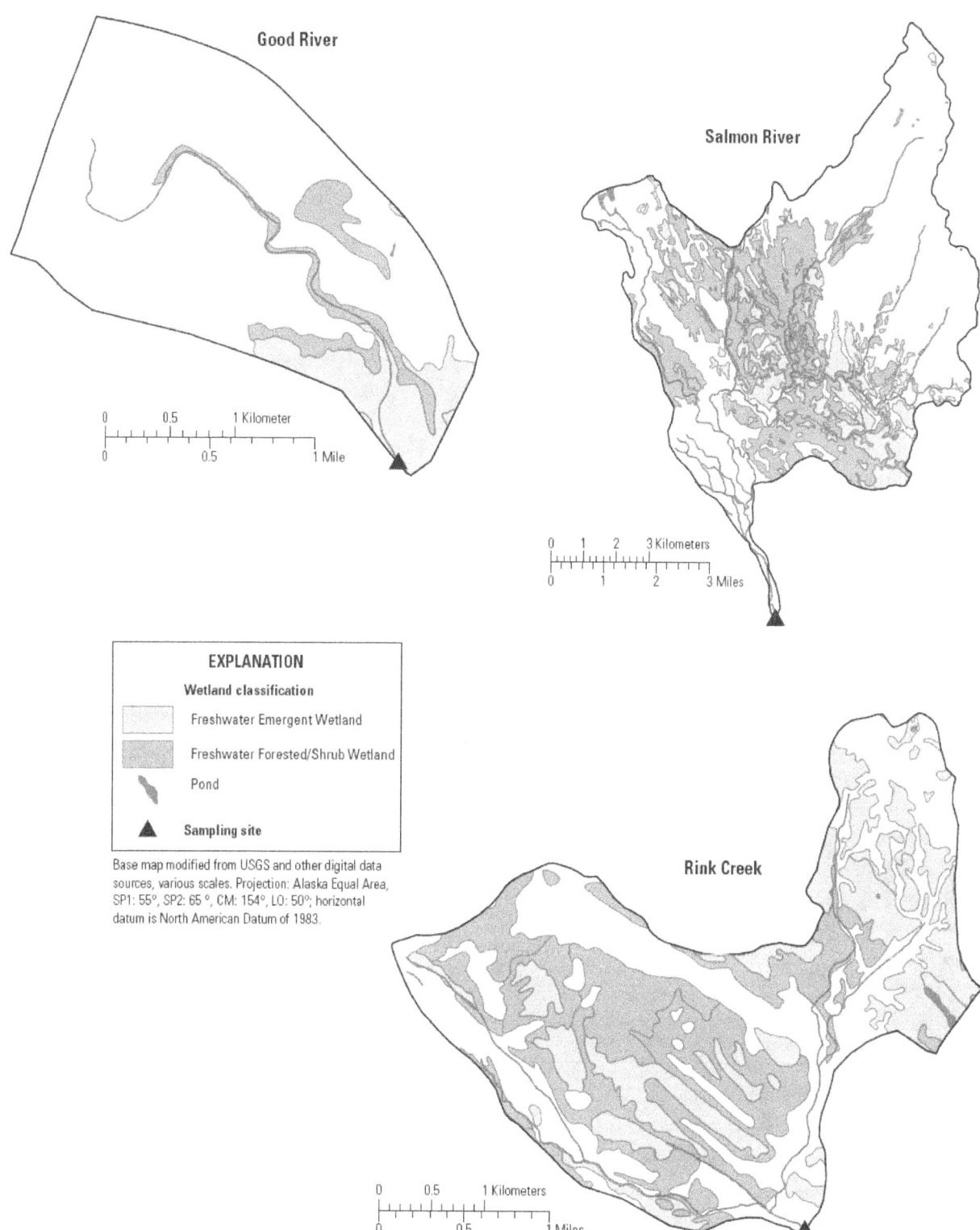

Figure 2. Wetland delineations within Rink Creek, Salmon River, and Good River watersheds, Glacier Bay National Park and Preserve, Alaska. (National Wetlands Inventory maps)

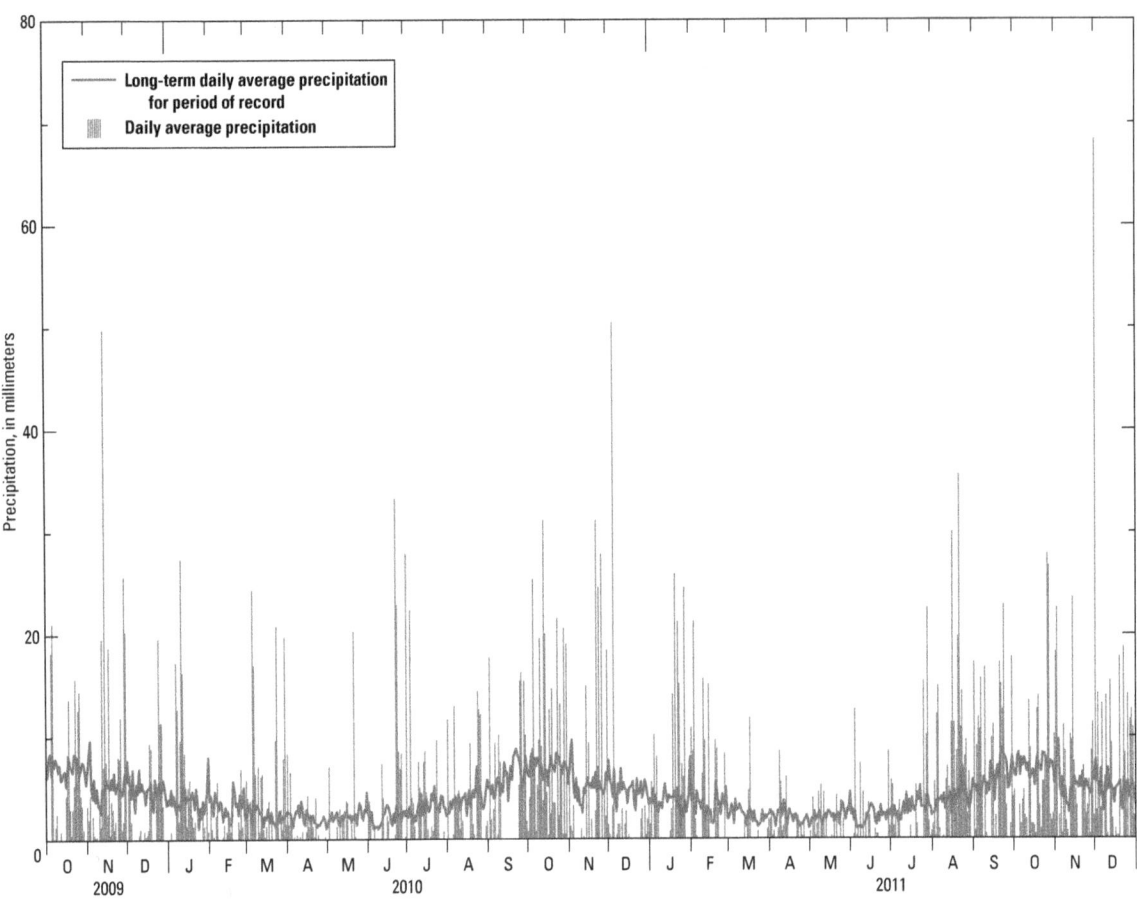

Figure 3.   Daily and long-term average precipitation for Gustavus, Alaska, October 2009–December 2011.

Table 1.   Physical characteristics of Rink Creek, Salmon River, and Good River watersheds, Glacier Bay National Park and Preserve, Alaska.

[Locations of sampling sites are shown in figure 1B. **Abbreviations:** km, kilometer; m, meter; NAD 83, North American Datum of 1983]

Site name	USGS site No.	Latitude (NAD 83)	Longitude (NAD 83)	Stream length (km)	Max watershed elevation (m)	Elevation at site (m)
Rink Creek	15057593	58°26'32"	135°40'24"	4.9	450	27.4
Salmon River	15057596	58°26'44"	135°44'25"	7.5	1,039	34.7
Good River	15057598	58°27'02"	135°47'17"	4.7	58	16.8

Table 2.   Watershed areas and wetland coverage of Rink Creek, Salmon River, and Good River, Glacier Bay National Park and Preserve, Alaska.

[Locations of sampling sites are shown in figure 1B. **Abbreviation:** km², square kilometer]

Site name	Area (km²)	Freshwater (km²)			Wetland total (percent of total area)
		Emergent wetland	Forested/ shrub wetland	Pond	
Rink Creek	16.9	4.38	5.54	0.00	59
Salmon River	86.0	9.50	22.61	0.23	37
Good River	6.1	0.65	0.49	0.00	19

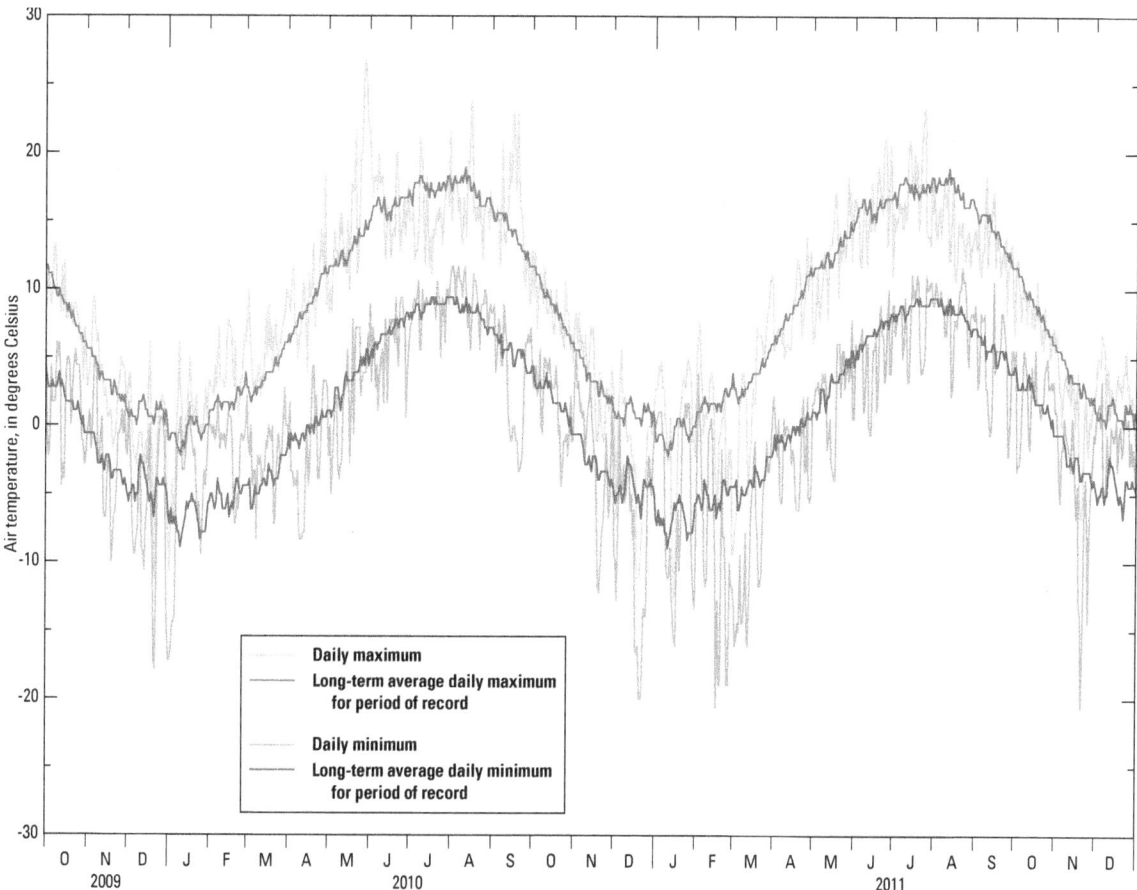

Figure 4.   Daily maximum and minimum air temperature and long-term average daily maximum and minimum air temperature for Gustavus, Alaska, October 2009–December 2011.

Local Atmospheric Mercury Deposition

During much of the study period, the National Park Service operated a Mercury Deposition Network (MDN) site in nearby Bartlett Cove (Station AK05), located 3–18 km from the study watersheds. Weekly wet deposition samples were collected following MDN procedures (http://nadp.sws.uiuc. edu/MDN/MDNfield.aspx) and analyzed for total mercury beginning in late March, 2010 (with 6 weeks of missing data). Data from these samples are available through the National Atmospheric Deposition Program (2012) and are listed in table 3.

Our compilation of the data provided at Bartlett Cove indicates that a weekly average of 50 nanograms per square meter (ng/m^2) of total Hg was deposited at the site when MDN collections overlapped with our study (March 2010–November 1, 2011). Mean Hg concentration was 2.94 nanograms per liter (ng/L) ($n=77$); however, volume-weighted concentrations were lower, with a mean of 1.56 ng/L.

Table 3. Mercury concentration in wet deposition and mercury deposition from weekly samples collected at the Mercury Deposition Network collection site at Bartlett Cove, Alaska, March 24, 2010, to November 1, 2011.

[**Abbreviations:** mm, millimeters; mL, milliliters; ng/L, nanograms per liter; ng/m^2, nanograms per square meter; –, missing data]

Date and Time	Precipitation (mm)	Sample volume (mL)	Mercury concentration (ng/L)	Mercury deposition (ng/m^2)
03-24-2010, 0230	44.5	418.1	0.95	42.2
03-30-2010, 2030	25.7	277.7	1.03	26.4
04-01-2010, 0230	1.3	–	–	–
04-06-2010, 2325	11.9	123.0	3.02	36.1
04-13-2010, 1757	6.1	49.4	2.46	15.0
04-21-2010, 0230	30.0	331.0	1.83	54.9
04-27-2010, 2110	8.1	83.3	6.66	54.1
05-05-2010, 0225	4.8	37.0	3.33	16.1
05-12-2010, 0010	1.5	12.8	10.75	16.4
05-18-2010, 1815	12.5	133.5	3.93	48.9
05-26-2010, 0005	2.3	10.8	15.04	34.4
06-01-2010, 1835	5.8	63.1	8.60	50.2
06-09-2010, 0200	6.1	75.6	3.15	19.2
06-16-2010, 0105	5.6	70.2	7.20	40.2
06-24-2010, 0440	68.6	796.3	1.27	87.1
06-29-2010, 2245	14.5	164.4	1.36	19.7
07-06-2010, 1925	53.9	620.7	1.72	92.6
07-13-2010, 1950	22.9	236.6	5.45	124.6
07-20-2010, 1820	12.7	141.6	3.44	43.7
07-27-2010, 1837	21.3	259.3	1.89	40.3
08-03-2010, 1750	9.7	109.2	2.28	22.0
08-10-2010, 2105	24.1	263.6	2.13	51.4
08-18-2010, 0120	5.1	52.7	4.83	24.5
08-24-2010, 2345	36.6	432.5	1.29	47.2
09-01-2010, 0210	25.9	269.7	2.54	65.8
09-07-2010, 2320	47.8	537.4	0.87	41.5
09-14-2010, 2050	9.9	125.6	2.71	26.9
09-28-2010, 2140	79.5	878.2	0.78	62.0
10-05-2010, 1825	84.8	1,035.7	0.75	63.6
10-13-2010, 0110	59.7	744.3	0.79	47.2
10-19-2010, 1815	102.1	1,275.7	–	–
10-27-2010, 0100	6.6	58.0	0.85	5.6
11-03-2010, 0210	69.3	826.0	0.76	52.7
11-10-2010, 0105	72.9	839.0	1.86	135.6
11-17-2010, 0140	63.3	716.9	0.81	51.2
11-23-2010, 1855	0.0	0.0	0.00	0.0
11-30-2010, 2300	59.9	697.9	1.10	65.9
12-07-2010, 2140	66.6	536.0	0.87	57.9
12-14-2010, 2350	12.2	128.7	1.31	16.0
01-04-2011, 2000	47.8	481.2	1.03	49.2

Table 3. Mercury concentration in wet deposition and mercury deposition from weekly samples collected at the Mercury Deposition Network collection site at Bartlett Cove, Alaska, March 24, 2010, to November 1, 2011.—Continued

[**Abbreviations:** mm, millimeters; mL, milliliters; ng/L, nanograms per liter; ng/m^2, nanograms per square meter; –, missing data]

Date and Time	Precipitation (mm)	Sample volume (mL)	Mercury concentration (ng/L)	Mercury deposition (ng/m^2)
01-11-2011, 1900	16.0	177.9	0.91	14.6
01-19-2011, 0050	16.3	56.9	3.16	51.4
01-26-2011, 1745	112.8	1,167.4	1.24	139.8
02-08-2011, 1905	59.2	659.1	1.50	88.8
02-15-2011, 2000	87.9	914.0	0.80	70.3
03-01-2011, 1930	5.6	7.8	10.40	58.2
03-17-2011, 2249	22.4	300.5	1.20	26.8
03-29-2011, 1815	2.3	9.3	6.53	14.9
04-05-2011, 2325	32.8	350.9	0.65	21.4
04-12-2011, 2030	46.2	511.1	0.95	43.9
04-20-2011, 0110	7.1	88.2	3.03	21.6
04-26-2011, 2145	7.6	49.2	2.70	20.6
05-04-2011, 0130	7.4	57.2	4.52	33.3
05-11-2011, 0120	45.2	447.0	1.41	64.0
05-18-2011, 0135	8.6	148.4	2.41	20.8
05-24-2011, 1855	15.2	142.7	6.89	105.1
06-01-2011, 0355	7.4	87.4	7.84	57.8
06-07-2011, 2250	5.1	42.0	11.11	56.5
06-14-2011, 1850	1.3	21.5	9.81	12.5
06-22-2011, 0150	4.8	35.3	1.78	8.6
06-29-2011, 0140	3.6	38.7	2.77	9.9
07-06-2011, 0155	23.6	258.2	2.64	62.4
07-13-2011, 0205	4.8	42.7	3.51	17.0
07-20-2011, 0050	6.1	64.9	2.39	14.6
07-26-2011, 2013	16.8	181.0	3.15	52.9
08-02-2011, 2143	25.2	282.9	1.37	34.7
08-09-2011, 2222	23.9	276.8	3.80	90.8
08-17-2011, 0050	85.9	1,015.4	1.06	91.0
08-24-2011, 0135	110.2	1,373.9	1.21	133.9
08-30-2011, 2250	42.7	470.9	1.36	58.1
09-07-2011, 0340	76.2	862.9	1.63	124.4
09-13-2011, 1645	23.9	304.7	2.43	58.1
09-20-2011, 2035	23.3	279.2	2.20	51.3
09-27-2011, 1830	66.6	738.6	1.06	71.0
10-04-2011, 2205	39.6	450.0	1.04	41.2
10-11-2011, 1825	17.0	166.1	1.80	30.7
10-18-2011, 2209	52.3	616.5	0.86	45.3
10-25-2011, 2125	33.8	360.9	1.13	38.4
11-01-2011, 2040	115.3	1,365.2	0.75	87.2

Field and Analytical Methods

Grab samples of water were collected at the same location at each stream 20 times between November 2009 and October 2011. Collection dates primarily were dictated by favorable weather conditions for flight access to the sites from Juneau, although generally we targeted one monthly sample during the first year and maximum hydrologic variability during the second year.

Hg and MeHg exposure in stream biota were assessed by collecting benthic macroinvertebrates (BMI) and resident fish. As primary consumers, BMI represent one of the lowest trophic levels for pollutants to enter into and biomagnify within aquatic food webs. Juvenile coho salmon that likely had not yet migrated out of their natal streams were targeted, with the aim of identifying a watershed-specific Hg signal in their tissues. Single streambed sediment samples also were collected at each stream site once in May 2010. Because streambed sediments, BMI, and fish are present together in small areas for extended periods of time, they integrate pollutants that may not be detected during standard water sampling, either because the pollutant is not present at detectable levels or is present intermittently (Krabbenhoft and others, 1999).

Water samples were collected by wading in the streams and using the best visual approximation of depth- and width-integrated conditions. Mercury water samples were collected in triple-rinsed, 2-L polyethylene terephthalate bottles, positioning the bottle upstream. The samples were then stored on ice, followed by clean filtration (through about 0.7 microgram [mm] ashed quartz fiber filters) and acidification (0.2 percent of sample volume) with ultraclean hydrochloric acid (HCl). Filtration was done the same day using a portable, metal-free filter apparatus. All pre-cleaned filtration equipment was provided by the USGS Mercury Research Laboratory (MRL) in Madison, Wisconsin. Particulate Hg was measured by analysis of filters through which 1 L of sample was passed. Additional water samples were filtered into amber glass bottles for dissolved organic carbon (DOC) analysis. Collection and processing procedures of samples for nutrients and major cations and anions followed USGS National Field Manual protocols (U.S. Geological Survey, variously dated).

Streambed sediment was collected by scraping several grams of the approximate top 1 cm of fine, unsieved sediment into a Teflon® vial. Mayfly nymphs or instars were dislodged from the streambed by foot and collected in a net. As many as 100 nymphs or instars from each family and stream were picked into a Teflon® vial. Seven to 10 juvenile coho salmon were captured at each site with a hand net or in baited minnow traps, and also were stored in small Teflon® vials. All samples were double-bagged, stored on ice, and handled by personnel wearing clean nitrile gloves. Sediment and biological specimens were frozen within 2 days. The age of

the juvenile coho salmon—likely either 1 or 2 years old—was not determined, although lengths were recorded; they were not young-of-the-year (fry), but, instead, were parr or smolts.

A Yellow Springs Instrument model 6920 multi-parameter sonde™ was used to measure water temperature, dissolved-oxygen concentration, specific conductance, turbidity, and pH at the time of sampling. The sonde was calibrated using known standards before sample collection. Discharge measurements, using a wading rod and Price current meter, also were made at the time of sampling following methods outlined by Turnipseed and Sauer (2010).

Analytical Methods for Mercury

All Hg analyses were done at the USGS MRL. Aqueous total Hg (Hg_T) analysis followed U.S. Environmental Protection Agency (USEPA) Method 1631 (U.S. Environmental Protection Agency, 2002). Aqueous MeHg analyses were performed following standard distillation and ethylation procedures described in detail elsewhere (Horvat and Bloom, 1993; DeWild and others, 2001), followed by analysis by cold-vapor atomic fluorescence spectrometry. Particulate, sediment, and biological tissue samples were analyzed for Hg_T and MeHg using the procedures described above; however, for each of these solid-phase samples, a solubilization step was first conducted to transform the sample into an aqueous state. For Hg_T in sediments and particulates, about 100 mg of homogenized, dried sample was digested in aqua regia (a mixture of nitric acid and hydrochloric acid) (Olund and others, 2004), whereas MeHg in sediment and particulates were solubilized with methylene chloride and heat (DeWild and others, 2004). Fish tissues and benthic invertebrates were digested in Teflon® bombs (a teflon container fitted in a steel jacket) using a concentrated mixture of nitric and sulfuric acids (5:2 volume-to-volume ratio) and were placed in an oven at 75°C for 2 hours. For MeHg solubilization of benthic invertebrates, a weak nitric acid method was used that included heating to 60°C in an oven and subsequent neutralization with potassium hydroxide (Hammerschmidt and Fitzgerald, 2006).

Quality Assurance for Mercury Analyses

Reference materials for Hg_T were within 97–103 percent (mean=100 percent, n=3) of the reported values for fish analyses, 85–115 percent (mean=93 percent, n=11) for macroinvertebrate analyses, 66–120 percent (mean=94 percent, n=35) for particulates, and 100–112 percent (mean=104 percent, n=5) for sediments. For MeHg, reference materials were recovered at 84–109 percent (mean=94 percent, n=9) for macroinvertebrates and 71–122 percent (mean=99 percent, n=15) for particulates.

The percent relative standard deviation of triplicate sample analyses of Hg_T and MeHg in biological tissues averaged 6.0 percent and 5.9 percent (n=6 for each), respectively, and 2.9 percent for triplicate runs of Hg_T in sediment. Each water sample was run in duplicate for Hg_T, and the average difference between runs was 0.6 percent (n=64). Spike recoveries on filtered Hg_T averaged 99.7 percent (n=47) and 103 percent (n=47) on filtered MeHg.

One field filtration blank was collected that was less than the detection limit for all mercury parameters: filtered total and MeHg, as well as particulate total and MeHg. In one sample (Salmon River, May 14, 2010), the filtered methylmercury (FMHg) value was greater than the filtered total mercury (FTHg) value; this sample was discarded from the dataset.

The mercury detection limit was between 1–2 nanograms per gram (ng/g) for benthic macroinvertebrates; 0.4–3.4 ng/g for fish samples; 0.02–0.1 ng/L for particulate Hg_T; 0.006 ng/L for particulate MeHg; 0.8 ng/g for sediment Hg_T; and between 0.02–0.04 ng/L for filtered Hg_T and MeHg.

Field duplicates of water samples were collected four times over the 2-year sampling period. The average discrepancy between the samples was 0.06 ng/L for filtered Hg_T; 0.01 ng/L for filtered MeHg; 0.27/ng L for particulate Hg_T; and 0.002 ng/L for particulate MeHg. A field duplicate of juvenile coho samples was collected from the Salmon River during the 2011 collection, and variation between samples was 5 percent for Hg_T and 8 percent for MeHg.

Analytical Methods for Other Water-Quality Parameters

DOC was measured within 2 days of receipt using the platinum catalyzed persulphate wet oxidation method (Aiken, 1992) on an O.I. Analytical Model 700 TOC Analyzer at the USGS National Research Program laboratory in Boulder, Colorado. Ultraviolet (UV)-Visible absorbance measurements were made on a Hewlett-Packard Model 8453™ photo-diode array spectrophotometer every 1 nanometer (nm) between 200 and 800 nm. Specific ultraviolet absorbance (SUVA) values (Weishaar and others, 2003), defined as the UV absorbance of the sample measured at a given wavelength divided by the DOC concentration, were calculated at 254 nm and are reported in units of liters per milligrams carbon times meter ([L/(mg C *m)]) by normalizing to a 1-m path length. Ultraviolet analyses were completed within 2 weeks of collection. Major ions and nutrients were analyzed at the USGS National Water Quality Laboratory in Denver, Colorado, using standard techniques (Fishman and Friedman, 1989).

Mercury and Water-Quality Data

The data have been compiled and are provided in tables 4–13. Field parameters collected at the time of sampling (discharge, pH, dissolved oxygen, and specific conductance), DOC, ultraviolet absorbance (UVA), and SUVA values are given in table 4. Filtered and particulate Hg_T and MeHg concentrations for the water samples are given in table 5. Note that concentrations for filtered methymercury (FMHg) and particulate methylmercury (PMHg) in a number of samples were less than the detection limit.

The instantaneous and specific fluxes for Hg_T and MeHg (filtered and particulate), and for DOC for each site are given in tables 6–8. Note that flux calculations were made only for samples with detectable mercury concentrations.

Concentrations of bed sediment, collected once on May 14, 2010, and analyzed for Hg_T, are given in table 9. The results of benthic macroinvertebrate sampling in 2010 and 2011 are shown in table 10. In 2010, the macroinvertebrates were analyzed only for MeHg, but in 2011, they were analyzed for MeHg and Hg_T. In 2010, two genera were collected: a caddisfly (*Onocosmoecus*, Limnephilidae) and a mayfly (*Baetis bicaudatus* and *B. tricaudatus,* Baetidae). In June 2011, the same two taxa were collected in the study streams, except *Baetis tricaudatus* was not found in Good River. Three additional mayfly taxa were collected in Rink Creek and Salmon River for Hg analyses: *Cinygmula, Ameletus,* and *Drunella grandis* (Ephemerellidae). The mayfly *Epeorus grandis* (Heptageniidae) was collected only in Salmon River in 2011 and was combined with the *Cinygmula* (Heptageniidae) sample.

The results of juvenile coho salmon sampling in 2010 and 2011 are shown in table 11. In 2010, samples were analyzed only for Hg_T, but in 2011, the samples were analyzed for MeHg and Hg_T. Note that the samples were of non-uniform length, and that the ages of fish were undetermined (length alone does not determine age and, therefore, does not determine mercury exposure).

Concentrations of major anions, cations, and nutrients were measured four times in 2010 to obtain background water-quality information on Rink Creek, Salmon River, and Good River. Results are provided in tables 12 and 13.

Table 4. Discharge, pH, dissolved oxygen, specific conductance, dissolved organic carbon, ultraviolet absorbance, and specific ultraviolet absorbance in water samples collected at Rink Creek, Salmon River, and Good River, Glacier Bay National Park and Preserve, Alaska, November 9, 2009, to October 26, 2011.

[The number in parentheses (below each constituent) is used by U.S. Environmental Protection Agency and U.S. Geological Survey to identify parameters in computerized databases. **Abbreviations:** Q, discharge; DO, dissolved oxygen; SC, specific conductance; DOC, dissolved organic carbon; UVA, ultraviolet absorbance; SUVA, specific ultraviolet absorbance; m³/s, cubic meters per second; mg/L, milligrams per liter; µS/cm, microsiemens per centimeter; nm, nanometer; L/mg C*m, liter per milligrams carbon times meter; NA, not available due to loss of sample or lack of measurement; E, estimated]

Date	Rink Creek Q (m³/s) (00061)	pH (units) (00400)	DO (mg/L) (00300)	SC (µS/cm) (00095)	DOC (mg/L) (00681)	UVA (254 nm) (50624)	SUVA (L/mg C*m) (63162)	Salmon River Q (m³/s) (00061)	pH (units) (00400)	DO (mg/L) (00300)	SC (µS/cm) (00095)	DOC (mg/L) (00681)	UVA (254 nm) (50624)	SUVA (L/mg C*m) (63162)	Good River Q (m³/s) (00061)	pH (units) (00400)	DO (mg/L) (00300)	SC (µS/cm) (00095)	DOC (mg/L) (00681)	UVA (254 nm) (50624)	SUVA (L/mg C*m) (63162)
11-09-2009	0.20	7.7	11.3	153	5.6	0.259	4.6	3.37	8.1	11.0	278	2.6	0.106	4	0.03	7.9	9.1	308	2.7	NA	NA
12-07-2009	0.19	7.1	12.4	173	4.8	0.195	4.1	1.98	7.6	11.4	397	2.2	0.07	3.1	0.03	7.4	10.4	301	2.8	NA	NA
01-26-2010	0.19	7.6	12.4	154	4.8	0.207	4.3	1.50	7.9	11.2	372	2	0.064	3.2	0.03	7.7	10.2	294	2.7	0.106	4
02-23-2010	0.22	7.3	12.7	142	5.2	0.217	4.2	1.98	7.8	11.7	307	2.2	0.082	3.7	0.03	7.5	9.7	292	2.7	0.147	5.4
03-16-2010	0.54	7.6	13.0	87	6.5	0.29	4.4	2.61	7.8	11.9	230	4.7	0.186	4	0.06	7.8	10.2	259	3	0.125	4.2
04-22-2010	0.65	7	11.8	69	7.9	NA	NA	6.23	7.6	12.0	140	4.1	NA	NA	0.06	7.5	8.9	269	2.4	NA	NA
05-14-2010	0.08	7.6	11.0	171	4.7	0.182	3.9	3.12	7.8	12.0	193	1.6	0.049	3.1	0.01	7.7	9.1	315	2.5	0.065	2.6
05-25-2010	0.05	7.6	10.1	205	4.6	0.199	4.3	4.59	7.9	11.9	154	1	0.033	3.4	0.01	7.7	8.4	307	2.7	0.098	3.6
06-10-2010	0.02	7.8	9.6	297	NA	NA	NA	2.27	7.9	11.2	199	NA	NA	NA	0.01	7.8	9.2	326	NA	NA	NA
07-26-2010	0.34	7.3	10.0	120	8.7	0.392	4.5	4.25	7.7	10.9	186	2.8	0.111	3.9	0.03	7.3	8.8	328	2.5	0.067	2.7
09-07-2010	0.31	7.9	9.4	138	9.5	0.413	4.3	2.58	8.2	10.0	246	4.1	0.163	3.9	0.03	7.9	7.7	340	2.6	0.089	3.4
10-06-2010	0.88	7.2	10.5	81	10.8	0.471	4.4	9.71	7.7	11.0	151	5.5	0.212	3.9	0.09	7.6	8.8	262	3.5	0.122	3.5
11-16-2010	0.42	7.4	11.9	137	7.2	0.29	4.1	4.02	7.8	11.4	305	3.1	0.095	3.1	0.05	7.6	9.8	285	3.4	0.133	3.9
01-11-2011	0.12	7.4	12.3	186	5.4	0.24	4.4	1.27	7.9	11.2	395	2.1	0.075	3.5	0.03	7.6	10.6	316	2.7	0.073	2.7
05-03-2011	0.57	7.1	12.3	75	NA	NA	NA	5.18	7.5	12.4	136	5.3	0.217	4.1	0.03	7.5	9.5	309	2.6	0.112	4.3
05-16-2011	0.27	7.3	10.9	119	6.3	0.292	4.6	4.76	7.6	12.1	187	1.8	0.076	4.2	0.03	7.4	8.9	312	2.2	0.097	4.5
06-21-2011	0.05	7.7	9.8	232	5.1	0.216	4.3	2.49	NA	11.1	216	1.1	0.035	3.1	0.01	7.6	9.3	332	2.4	0.064	2.6
07-26-2011	0.82	7.2	10.6	62	14.6	0.657	4.5	3.29	7.5	10.2	119	8.9	0.373	4.2	0.03	7.4	8.4	342	NA	NA	NA
09-22-2011	2.41	6.2	10.2	55	12	0.553	4.6	16.65	6.9	10.9	107	7.6	0.348	4.6	0.19	7.4	9.1	223	3.7	0.122	3.3
10-26-2011	E4.8	NA	NA	NA	10.6	0.485	4.6	E33.3	NA	NA	NA	8.6	0.379	4.4	E0.37	NA	NA	NA	3.0	0.086	2.8

Table 5. Filtered and particulate total mercury and methylmercury concentrations, and the percent of total mercury occurring in the filtered phase, in water samples collected at Rink Creek, Salmon River, and Good River, Glacier Bay National Park and Preserve, Alaska, November 9, 2009, to October 26, 2011.

[The number in parentheses (below each constituent) is used by U.S. Environmental Protection Agency and U.S. Geological Survey to identify parameters in computerized databases. Values in *italic* indicate that concentration is less than the detection limit of 0.04 ng/L. **Abbreviations:** FTHg, filtered total mercury; FMHg, filtered methylmercury; PTHg, particulate total mercury; PMHg, particulate methylmercury; Hg_T, total mercury; ng/L, nanogram per liter; NA, not available due to loss of sample or lack of collection; E, estimated; <, less than]

Date	Rink Creek					Salmon River					Good River				
	FTHg (ng/L) (50287)	FMHg (ng/L) (50285)	PTHg (ng/L) (62976)	PMHg (ng/L) (62977)	Hg_T filtered (percent)	FTHg (ng/L) (50287)	FMHg (ng/L) (50285)	PTHg (ng/L) (62976)	PMHg (ng/L) (62977)	Hg_T filtered (percent)	FTHg (ng/L) (50287)	FMHg (ng/L) (50285)	PTHg (ng/L) (62976)	PMHg (ng/L) (62977)	Hg_T filtered (percent)
11-09-2009	1.24	*<0.04*	0.42	0.01	75	0.59	*<0.04*	0.09	<0.008	87	0.15	*<0.04*	0.10	0.08	60
12-07-2009	0.98	*<0.04*	0.23	0.01	81	0.45	*<0.04*	0.07	<0.008	87	0.17	*<0.04*	0.21	<0.008	44
01-26-2010	1.15	0.14	0.19	0.01	86	1.62	*<0.04*	0.12	<0.008	93	0.32	*<0.04*	<0.087	<0.014	88
02-23-2010	1.80	0.04	0.34	<0.008	84	0.59	*<0.04*	0.14	<0.010	81	0.50	*<0.04*	0.11	<0.007	82
03-16-2010	2.13	*<0.04*	0.37	NA	85	1.48	*<0.04*	0.11	NA	93	1.12	*<0.04*	0.20	<0.009	85
04-22-2010	2.29	0.05	0.21	NA	92	1.40	*<0.04*	0.34	NA	80	0.29	*<0.04*	0.75	NA	28
05-14-2010	1.12	0.04	0.16	<0.009	88	0.56	NA	0.10	<0.010	85	0.30	*<<0.04*	0.08	<0.010	79
05-25-2010	1.09	*<0.04*	0.10	NA	92	0.31	*<0.04*	0.09	<0.009	78	0.23	*<0.04*	0.09	<0.008	71
06-10-2010	0.76	0.04	0.12	0.01	87	0.33	*<0.04*	0.11	<0.009	75	0.17	*<0.04*	<0.061	<0.009	85
07-26-2010	2.10	0.09	0.60	<0.009	78	0.95	*<0.04*	0.30	<0.008	76	0.24	*<0.04*	0.58	NA	29
09-07-2010	1.85	0.16	0.47	0.01	80	1.10	0.05	0.28	<0.009	80	0.63	*<0.04*	0.26	<0.011	71
10-06-2010	2.49	0.09	0.91	0.01	73	1.50	0.05	0.66	<0.010	69	0.41	0.04	0.64	0.01	39
11-16-2010	1.48	0.05	0.23	<0.009	86	0.69	*<0.04*	0.20	<0.010	77	0.28	0.08	0.25	<0.009	53
01-11-2011	1.06	0.09	0.26	<0.007	81	0.49	*<0.04*	0.10	<0.009	83	0.19	*<0.04*	0.15	<0.010	56
05-03-2011	2.53	*<0.04*	0.81	0.01	76	1.81	*<0.04*	1.09	0.02	62	0.09	*<0.04*	0.65	0.01	12
05-16-2011	2.70	0.14	0.67	<0.010	80	1.03	*<0.04*	0.72	<0.009	59	0.42	*<0.04*	0.92	<0.009	31
06-21-2011	1.23	*<0.04*	E0.064	0.02	95	0.44	0.04	E0.089	<0.008	83	0.24	*<0.04*	0.25	<0.009	49
07-26-2011	3.93	0.05	1.00	0.02	80	2.48	*<0.04*	0.46	0.02	84	0.17	*<0.04*	0.21	<0.010	45
09-22-2011	3.87	*<0.04*	0.70	0.01	85	2.92	*<0.04*	0.83	0.01	78	0.55	*<0.04*	0.35	<0.006	61
10-26-2011	3.53	0.04	1.33	0.02	73	3.93	0.06	3.64	0.01	52	0.36	*<0.04*	0.60	<0.006	38

Table 6.   Instantaneous flux and specific flux for total mercury and methylmercury in the filtered and particulate phase, and dissolved organic carbon flux and specific flux for Rink Creek, Glacier Bay National Park and Preserve, Alaska, November 9, 2009, to October 26, 2011.

[**Abbreviations:** FTHg, filtered total mercury; FMHg, filtered methylmercury; PTHg, particulate total mercury; PMHg, particulate methylmercury; sp flux, specific flux; ng/s, nanograms per second; (ng/s)/km^2, nanograms per second per square kilometer; BDL, below detection limit; NA, not available due to loss of sample or lack of collection; E, estimated]

Date	FTHg flux (ng/s)	FTHg sp flux [(ng/s)/km^2]	FMHg flux (ng/s)	FMHg sp flux [(ng/s)/km^2]	PTHg flux (ng/s)	PTHg sp flux [(ng/s)/km^2]	PMHg flux (ng/s)	PMHg sp flux [(ng/s)/km^2]	DOC flux (ng/s)	DOC sp flux (ng/s/km^2)
11-09-2009	246	19	BDL	BDL	82	6	2.4	0.2	1,110	86
12-07-2009	183	14	BDL	BDL	42	3	2.6	0.2	897	69
01-26-2010	215	17	26	2	36	3	1.7	0.1	897	69
02-23-2010	398	31	9	1	76	6	BDL	BDL	1,149	89
03-16-2010	1,146	88	BDL	BDL	196	15	BDL	BDL	3,497	270
04-22-2010	1,491	115	33	3	135	10	BDL	BDL	5,145	397
05-14-2010	92	7	3	0.3	13	1	BDL	BDL	386	30
05-25-2010	59	5	BDL	BDL	5	0.4	BDL	BDL	247	19
06-10-2010	19	1	1	0.1	3	0.2	0.2	0.0	NA	NA
07-26-2010	714	55	31	2	204	16	BDL	BDL	2,956	228
09-07-2010	576	44	50	4	146	11	3.4	0.3	2,959	229
10-06-2010	2,186	169	79	6	794	61	9.7	0.7	9,480	732
11-16-2010	629	49	21	2	99	8	BDL	BDL	3,058	236
01-11-2011	126	10	11	1	30	2	BDL	BDL	642	50
05-03-2011	1,433	111	BDL	BDL	460	36	7.9	0.6	NA	NA
05-16-2011	726	56	38	3	179	14	BDL	BDL	1,695	131
06-21-2011	66	5	BDL	BDL	BDL	BDL	0.9	0.1	274	21
07-26-2011	3,227	249	41	3	821	63	19.7	1.5	11,989	926
09-22-2011	9,315	719	BDL	BDL	1,673	129	28.9	2.2	28,883	2,230
10-26-2011	E17,000	E1,300	E190	E15	E6,400	E500	E90	E7.1	E51,000	E4,000

Table 7.   Instantaneous flux and specific flux for total mercury and methylmercury in the filtered and particulate phase, and dissolved organic carbon flux and specific flux for Salmon River, Glacier Bay National Park and Preserve, Alaska, November 9, 2009, to October 26, 2011.

[**Abbreviations:** FTHg, filtered total mercury; FMHg, filtered methylmercury; PTHg, particulate total mercury; PMHg, particulate methylmercury; sp flux, specific flux; ng/s, nanograms per second; (ng/s)/km^2, nanograms per second per square kilometer; BDL, below detection limit; NA, not available due to loss of sample or lack of collection; E, estimated]

Date	FTHg flux (ng/s)	FTHg sp flux [(ng/s)/km^2]	FMHg flux (ng/s)	FMHg sp flux [(ng/s)/km^2]	PTHg flux (ng/s)	PTHg sp flux [(ng/s)/km^2]	PMHg flux (ng/s)	PMHg sp flux [(ng/s)/km^2]	DOC flux (ng/s)	DOC sp flux [(ng/s)/km^2]
11-09-2009	1,988	34	BDL	BDL	310	24	BDL	BDL	8,761	677
12-07-2009	892	15	BDL	BDL	135	10	BDL	BDL	4,361	337
01-26-2010	2,431	42	BDL	BDL	180	14	BDL	BDL	3,002	232
02-23-2010	1,169	20	BDL	BDL	278	21	BDL	BDL	4,361	337
03-16-2010	3,856	66	BDL	BDL	289	22	NA	NA	12,244	945
04-22-2010	8,722	150	BDL	BDL	2,118	164	NA	NA	25,542	1,972
05-14-2010	1,744	30	NA	NA	318	25	BDL	BDL	4,984	385
05-25-2010	1,422	25	BDL	BDL	395	30	BDL	BDL	4,587	354
06-10-2010	748	13	BDL	BDL	249	19	BDL	BDL	BDL	BDL
07-26-2010	4,035	70	BDL	BDL	1,291	100	BDL	BDL	11,893	918
09-07-2010	2,835	49	129	10	724	56	BDL	BDL	10,565	816
10-06-2010	14,569	251	486	38	6,449	498	BDL	BDL	53,420	4,125
11-16-2010	2,774	48	BDL	BDL	820	63	BDL	BDL	12,465	963
01-11-2011	624	11	BDL	BDL	127	10	BDL	BDL	2,676	207
05-03-2011	9,379	162	BDL	BDL	5,648	436	88	2	27,465	2,121
05-16-2011	4,900	84	BDL	BDL	3,435	265	BDL	BDL	8,563	661
06-21-2011	1,096	19	100	8	E222	E17	BDL	BDL	2,741	212
07-26-2011	8,146	140	BDL	BDL	1,524	118	55.8	1.0	29,234	2,257
09-22-2011	48,619	838	BDL	BDL	13,803	1,066	216.5	3.7	126,542	9,772
10-26-2011	E131,000	E2,260	E2,000	E150	E121,000	E9,400	E430	E8	E290,000	E22,000

Table 8. Instantaneous flux and specific flux for total mercury and methylmercury in the filtered and particulate phase, and dissolved organic carbon flux and specific flux for Good River, Glacier Bay National Park and Preserve, Alaska, November 9, 2009, to October 26, 2011.

[**Abbreviations:** FTHg, filtered total mercury; FMHg, filtered methylmercury; PTHg, particulate total mercury; PMHg, particulate methylmercury; sp flux, specific flux; ng/s, nanograms per second; (ng/s)/km², nanograms per second per square kilometer; BDL, below detection limit; NA, not available due to loss of sample or lack of collection; E, estimated]

Date	FTHg flux (ng/s)	FTHg sp flux [(ng/s)/km²]	FMHg flux (ng/s)	FMHg sp flux [(ng/s)/km²]	PTHg flux (ng/s)	PTHg sp flux [(ng/s)/km²]	PMHg flux (ng/s)	PMHg sp flux [(ng/s)/km²]	DOC flux (ng/s)	DOC sp flux [(ng/s)/km²]
11-09-2009	4.7	0.8	BDL	BDL	3.2	0.2	2.4	0.4	84.1	6.5
12-07-2009	5.3	0.9	BDL	BDL	6.6	0.5	BDL	BDL	87.2	6.7
01-26-2010	10.0	1.7	BDL	BDL	BDL	BDL	BDL	BDL	74.9	5.8
02-23-2010	15.6	2.6	BDL	BDL	3.3	0.3	BDL	BDL	84.1	6.5
03-16-2010	34.9	5.9	BDL	BDL	12.5	1.0	BDL	BDL	186.9	14.4
04-22-2010	9.0	1.5	BDL	BDL	44.8	3.5	NA	NA	142.7	11.0
05-14-2010	9.3	1.6	BDL	BDL	1.0	0.1	BDL	BDL	31.9	2.5
05-25-2010	7.2	1.2	BDL	BDL	0.8	0.1	BDL	BDL	23.7	1.8
06-10-2010	5.3	0.9	BDL	BDL	BDL	BDL	BDL	BDL	NA	NA
07-26-2010	7.5	1.3	BDL	BDL	19.7	1.5	NA	NA	85.0	6.6
09-07-2010	19.6	3.3	BDL	BDL	8.2	0.6	BDL	BDL	81.0	6.3
10-06-2010	12.8	2.1	3.5	0.3	56.4	4.4	1.0	0.2	307.2	23.7
11-16-2010	8.7	1.5	4.3	0.3	13.5	1.0	BDL	BDL	182.9	14.1
01-11-2011	5.9	1.0	BDL	BDL	4.0	0.3	BDL	BDL	70.3	5.4
05-03-2011	2.8	0.5	BDL	BDL	20.2	1.6	0.4	0.1	81.0	6.3
05-16-2011	13.1	2.2	BDL	BDL	24.5	1.9	BDL	BDL	58.6	4.5
06-21-2011	7.5	1.3	BDL	BDL	2.1	0.2	BDL	BDL	19.7	1.5
07-26-2011	5.3	0.9	BDL	BDL	5.4	0.4	BDL	BDL	NA	NA
09-22-2011	17.1	2.9	BDL	BDL	64.5	5.0	BDL	BDL	691.5	53.4
10-26-2011	E11	E2	BDL	BDL	E220	E17	BDL	BDL	E1,100	E87

Table 9. Concentrations of total mercury in streambed sediments collected at Rink Creek, Salmon River, and Good River, Glacier Bay National Park and Preserve, Alaska, May 24, 2010.

[**Abbreviation:** ng/g, nanograms per gram, dry weight]

Site name	Total mercury (ng/g)
Rink Creek	35.5
Salmon River	19.6
Good River	9.9

Table 10.   Taxonomy, trophic position, and mercury concentrations in benthic macroinvertebrates from Rink Creek, Salmon River, and Good River, Glacier Bay National Park and Preserve, Alaska, 2010 and 2011.

[**Trophic position:** Sh, shredder; C-G, collector-gatherer; Sc, scraper; P, predator. **MeHg:** percentage of total mercury as methylmercury. **Abbreviations:** BMHg, biota methylmercury; BTHg, biota total mercury; ng/g, nanograms per gram; –, no data]

Sample date	Group	Order	Family	Genus	Species	Trophic position	BMHg (ng/g)	BTHg (ng/g)	MeHg (percent)
				Rink Creek					
05-25-2010	Caddisfly	Trichoptera	Limnephilidae	*Onocosmoecus*	–	Sh	11.4	–	–
06-21-2011	Caddisfly	Trichoptera	Limnephilidae	*Onocosmoecus*	–	Sh	18.0	32.7	55
06-21-2011	Mayfly	Ephemeroptera	Ameletidae	*Ameletus*	–	C-G	96.9	138	70
05-25-2010	Mayfly	Ephemeroptera	Baetidae	*Baetis*	*tricaudatus+bicaudatus*	C-G	52.7	–	–
06-21-2011	Mayfly	Ephemeroptera	Baetidae	*Baetis*	*tricaudatus+bicaudatus*	C-G	32.7	72.3	45
06-21-2011	Mayfly	Ephemeroptera	Heptageniidae	*Cinygmula*	–	C-G	92.0	171	54
06-21-2011	Mayfly	Ephemeroptera	Ephemerellidae	*Drunella*	*grandis*	Sc, P	96.2	146	66
				Salmon River					
05-25-2010	Caddisfly	Trichoptera	Limnephilidae	*Onocosmoecus*	–	Sh	8.8	–	–
06-21-2011	Caddisfly	Trichoptera	Limnephilidae	*Onocosmoecus*	–	Sh	14.9	49.7	30
06-21-2011	Mayfly	Ephemeroptera	Ameletidae	*Ameletus*	–	C-G	36.6	96.1	38
05-25-2010	Mayfly	Ephemeroptera	Baetidae	*Baetis*	*bicaudatus*	C-G	28.2	–	–
06-21-2011	Mayfly	Ephemeroptera	Baetidae	*Baetis*	*bicaudatus*	C-G	45.8	119	38
06-21-2011	Mayfly	Ephemeroptera	Heptageniidae	*Cinygmula+Epeorus grandis*	–	C-G	77.3	140	55
06-21-2011	Mayfly	Ephemeroptera	Ephemerellidae	*Drunella*	*grandis*	Sc, P	48.1	109	44
				Good River					
05-25-2010	Caddisfly	Trichoptera	Limnephilidae	*Onocosmoecus*	–	Sh	5.9	–	–
06-21-2011	Caddisfly	Trichoptera	Limnephilidae	–	–	Sh	11.2	23.2	48
05-25-2010	Mayfly	Ephemeroptera	Baetidae	*Baetis*	*tricaudatus*	C-G	9.3	–	–

Table 11.   Methylmercury and total mercury concentrations (wet weight and dry weight) in juvenile coho salmon samples from Rink Creek, Salmon River, and Good River, Glacier Bay National Park and Preserve, Alaska, 2010 and 2011.

[**MeHg:** percent of total mercury as methylmercury. **Abbreviations:** mm, millimeters; BMHg, biota methylmercury; BTHg, biota total mercury; std dev, standard deviation; ng/g dw, nanograms per gram dry weight; ng/g ww, nanograms per gram wet weight; NA, not analyzed; –, no data]

Site name	Sample date	Sample size	Fish length (mm) mean (std dev)	BMHg (ng/g dw)	BMHg (ng/g ww)	BTHg (ng/g dw)	BTHg (ng/g ww)	MeHg (percent)
Rink Creek	05-14-2010	8	99 (5)	(NA)	(NA)	112	24.4	–
	05-17-2011	10	64 (8)	236	51.4	281	61.2	84
Salmon River	05-14-2010	8	82 (3)	(NA)	(NA)	226	45.5	–
	05-17-2011	9	68 (9)	179	37.6	209	43.9	86
Good River	05-14-2010	8	98 (8)	(NA)	(NA)	157	34.2	–
	05-17-2011	9	100 (15)	119	25.0	176	37.0	68

Table 12. Concentrations of total dissolved solids, major anions, and major cations from water samples collected at Rink Creek, Salmon River, and Good River, Glacier Bay National Park and Preserve, Alaska, 2010.

[The number in parentheses (below each constituent) is used by U.S. Environmental Protection Agency and U.S. Geological Survey to identify parameters in computerized databases. **Abbreviations:** mg/L, milligrams per liter; E, estimated; <, less than]

Date	Dissolved solids (mg/L) (70300)	Calcium (mg/L) (00915)	Magnesium (mg/L) (00925)	Potassium (mg/L) (00935)	Sodium (mg/L) (00930)	Alkalinity (mg/L) (29801)	Chloride (mg/L) (00940)	Flouride (mg/L) (00950)	Silica (mg/L) (00955)	Sulfate (mg/L) (00945)
				Rink Creek						
04-22-2010	55	11	0.838	0.32	2.56	31.8	3.54	<0.08	2.45	0.75
09-07-2010	104	21.9	1.72	0.7	4.76	60.8	7.25	<0.08	4.44	1.03
10-06-2010	67	13	1.01	0.6	2.83	36.4	4.89	<0.040	3.06	0.78
11-16-2010	90	21.2	1.68	0.58	5.14	59.6	8.44	<0.04	4.36	1.26
				Salmon River						
04-22-2010	88	23.1	1.99	0.56	3.75	64.5	5.37	<0.08	2.65	4.02
09-07-2010	149	35.9	3.93	1.21	10.3	101	16.4	<0.08	4.44	5.52
10-06-2010	110	26.2	2.28	0.64	3.49	70.9	5.34	<0.04	3.14	4.61
11-16-2010	170	39.5	4.94	1.46	16.1	109	26.6	0.04	4.83	6.92
				Good River						
04-22-2010	175	51.8	2.86	1.62	2.5	152	2.36	E0.04	7.84	0.52
09-07-2010	198	65.5	4.34	1.94	3.42	186	2.79	<0.08	10.6	0.38
10-06-2010	173	51.6	2.42	1.52	1.97	148	2.69	<0.04	7.18	0.38
11-16-2010	162	57	3.15	1.52	2.41	159	2.2	0.05	8.52	0.42

Table 13. Concentrations of ammonia, nitrogen and phosphorus species, dissolved iron, and dissolved manganese from water samples collected at Rink Creek, Salmon River, and Good River, Glacier Bay National Park and Preserve, Alaska, 2010.

[The number in parentheses (below each constituent) is used by U.S. Environmental Protection Agency and U.S. Geological Survey to identify parameters in computerized databases. **Abbreviations:** N, nitrogen; P, phosphorus; mg/L, milligrams per liter; µg/L, micrograms per liter; E, estimated; <, less than; −, no data]

Date	Ammonia + org -N dissolved (as N) (mg/L) (00623)	Ammonia + org -N, total (as N) (mg/L) (00625)	Ammonia, dissolved (as N) (mg/L) (00608)	Nitrate + nitrite, dissolved (as N) (mg/L) (00631)	Nitrite, dissolved (as N) (mg/L) (00613)	Ortho-phosphate, dissolved (as P) (mg/L) (00671)	Phosphorus, dissolved (as P) (mg/L) (00666)	Phosphorus, total (as P) (mg/L) (00665)	Iron, dissolved (µg/L) (01046)	Manganese, dissolved (µg/L) (01056)
					Rink Creek					
04-22-2010	0.12	0.12	E0.011	<0.016	E0.001	<0.008	E0.007	−	219	19.4
09-07-2010	0.21	0.19	<0.020	<0.016	E0.001	E0.008	0.007	0.13	553	79.5
10-06-2010	0.2	0.24	<0.010	<0.008	<0.001	<0.004	0.005	0.013	344	24.2
11-16-2010	0.13	0.12	0.017	0.011	0.001	0.008	0.009	0.011	377	48.7
					Salmon River					
04-22-2010	E0.08	E0.07	<0.020	0.123	<0.002	E 0.005	E0.004	E0.006	78.9	9.38
09-07-2010	0.13	E0.10	E0.017	0.05	E0.001	0.01	0.009	0.012	118	28.9
10-06-2010	0.11	0.12	<0.010	0.07	<0.001	<0.004	0.003	0.009	102	8.23
11-16-2010	0.11	0.09	0.035	0.101	<0.001	0.01	0.01	0.011	81.9	25.6
					Good River					
04-22-2010	E0.08	E0.09	E0.013	<0.016	<0.002	E0.007	E0.003	0.029	255	119
09-07-2010	E0.09	E0.05	<0.020	<0.016	<0.002	0.009	<0.006	0.019	24.1	221
10-06-2010	0.14	0.15	<0.010	<0.008	<0.001	0.007	0.007	0.024	197	72.7
11-16-2010	0.11	0.08	<0.010	<0.008	<0.001	0.007	<0.003	0.015	107	132

Acknowledgments

The authors wish to thank the following people for their efforts in this project. John Hudson (independent aquatic ecologist) assisted in the collection and identification of the benthic macroinvertebrates. Kenna Butler of the USGS National Research Program processed the DOC, UVA, and SUVA samples. John DeWild of the USGS Mercury Research Laboratory processed all mercury samples. Chad Soiseth of Glacier Bay National Park and Preserve arranged logistics for sampling crews traveling to Gustavus and collected samples during the high-flow event on October 26, 2011.

References Cited

Aiken, G.R., 1992, Chlorine interference in the analysis of dissolved organic carbon by the wet oxidation method: Environmental Science and Technology, v. 26, no. 12, p. 2,435–2,439.

Alaska Department of Fish and Game, 2005, Catalog of waters important for spawning, rearing or migration of anadromous fishes: Juneau, Alaska Department of Fish and Game, 205 p.

Bradsher, Keith, and Barboza, David, 2006, Pollution from Chinese coal casts a global shadow: New York, New York Times article, June 16, 2006.

Brew, D.A., 2008, Delineation of landform and lithologic units for ecological landtype-association analysis in Glacier Bay National Park, southeast Alaska: U.S. Geological Survey Scientific Investigations Report 2008-5183, 7 p. (Also available at http://pubs.usgs.gov/sir/2008/5183/.)

Connor, C.L., Streveler, G.P., Post, A., Monteith, D., and Howell, W., 2009, The neoglacial landscape and human history of Glacier Bay, Glacier Bay National Park and Preserve, southeast Alaska, USA: The Holocene, v. 19, no. 3, p. 381–393.

Dastoor, A.P., and Larocque, Y., 2004, Global circulation of atmospheric mercury—A modelling study: Atmospheric Environment, v. 38, p. 147–161.

Day, R.D., Vander Pol, S.S., Christopher, S.J., Davis, W.C., Pugh, R.S., Simac, K., Roseneau, D.G., and Becker, P.R., 2006, Murre eggs (Uria aalge and Uria lomvia) as indicators of mercury contamination in the Alaskan marine environment: Environmental Science and Technology, v. 40, no. 3, p. 659–665.

DeWild, J.F., Olson, M.L., and Olund, S.D., 2001, Determination of methyl mercury by aqueous phase ethylation, followed by gas chromatographic separation with cold vapor atomic fluorescence detection: U.S. Geological Survey Open-File Report 2001-445, 14 p. (Also available at http://pubs.usgs.gov/of/2001/ofr-01-445/.)

DeWild, J.F., Olund, S.D., Olson, M.L., and Tate, M.T., 2004, Methods for the preparation and analysis of solids and suspended solids for methylmercury: U.S. Geological Survey Techniques and Methods, book 5, chap. A7, 13 p. (Also available at http://pubs.usgs.gov/tm/2005/tm5A7/.)

Engstrom, D.R., and Swain, E.B., 1997, Recent declines in atmospheric mercury deposition in the upper midwest: Environmental Science and Technology, v. 31, p. 960–967.

Fellman, J.B., D'Amore, D.V., Hood, Eran, and Boone, R.D., 2007, Fluorescence characteristics and biodegradability of dissolved organic matter in forest and wetland soils from coastal temperate watersheds in southeast Alaska: Biogeochemistry, v. 88, no. 2, p. 169–184, DOI 10.1007/s10533-008-9203-x.

Fishman, M.J., and Friedman, L.C., eds., 1989, Methods for determination of inorganic substances in water and fluvial sediments (3d. ed.), U.S. Geological Survey Techniques of Water-Resources Investigations, book 5, chap. A1, p. 545. (Also available at http://pubs.usgs.gov/twri/twri5-a1/.)

Fitzgerald, W.F., Engstrom, D.R., Lamborg, C.H., Tseng, C.M., Balcom, P.H., and Hammerschmidt, C.R., 2005, Modern and historic atmospheric mercury fluxes in northern Alaska—Global source and arctic depletion: Environmental Science and Technology, v. 39, p. 557–568.

Fitzgerald, W.F., Engstrom, D.R., Mason, R.P., and Nater, E.A., 1998, The case for atmospheric mercury contamination in remote areas: Environmental Science and Technology v. 32, p. 1–7.

Hammerschmidt, C.R., and Fitzgerald, W.F., 2006, Bioaccumulation and trophic transfer of methylmercury in Long Island Sound: Archives of Environmental Contamination and Toxicology, v. 51, p. 416–424.

Horvat, M., and Bloom, N.S., 1993, Comparison of distillation with other current isolation methods for the determination of methyl mercury compounds in low level environmental samples—Part 1, Sediments: Analytica Chimica Acta, v. 281, no. 1, p. 135–152.

Krabbenhoft, D.P., Wiener, J.G., Brumbaugh, W.G., Olson, M.L., DeWild, J.F., and Sabin, T.J., 1999, A national pilot study of mercury contamination of aquatic ecosystems along multiple gradients: U.S. Geological Survey Biological Science Report 2001-0009, 25 p.

Nagorski, S.A., Engstrom, D.E., Hudson, John, Krabbenhoft, D.P., DeWild, J.F., Hood, Eran, and Aiken, G.R., 2011, Scale and distribution of global pollutants in Southeast Alaska Network park watersheds: Natural Resource Technical Report NPS/SEAN/NRTR—2011/496, 67 p., accessed March 6, 2013, at http://science.nature nps.gov/im/units/sean/auxrep/FC/FC_Nagorski%20NRTR%202011-496.pdf.

National Atmospheric Deposition Program, 2012, Mercury Deposition Network: National Atmospheric Deposition Program web site, accessed November 14, 2012, at http://nadp.sws.uiuc.edu/mdn/.

National Oceanic Atmospheric Association, variously dated, National Weather Service Climate station Gustavus, Alaska, accessed August 15, 2012 at http://www.wrcc.dri.edu/summary/Climsmak.html.

Nriagu, J.G., and Pacyna, J.M., 1988, Quantitative assessment of worldwide contamination of air, water, and soils with trace metals: Nature, v. 333, p. 134–139.

Olund, S.D., DeWild, J.F., Olson, M.L., and Tate, M.T., 2004, Methods for the preparation and analysis of solids and suspended solids for total mercury: U.S. Geological Survey Techniques and Methods book 5, chap. A8, 15 p. (Also available at http://pubs.usgs.gov/tm/2005/tm5A8/.)

Pacyna, E.G., Pacyna, J.M., Sundseth, K., Munthe, J., Kindbom, K., Wilson, S., Steenhuisen, F., and Maxon, P., 2010, Global emission of mercury to the atmosphere from anthropogenic sources in 2005 and projections to 2020: Atmospheric Environment, v. 44, p. 2487–2499.

Rossman, D.L., 1963, Geology of the eastern part of the Mount Fairweather quadrangle, Glacier Bay, Alaska: U.S. Geological Survey Bulletin, v. 1121-K, p. 1–57.

Schroeder, W.H., and Munthe, J., 1998, Atmospheric mercury—An overview: Atmospheric Environment, v. 32, p. 809–822.

Streveler, G.P., 1996, The natural history of Gustavus: G. Streveler, 53 p.

Sunderland, E.M., Krabbenhoft, D.P., Moreau, J.W., Strode, S.A., and Landing, W.M., 2009, Mercury sources, distribution, and bioavailability in the North Pacific Ocean—Insights from data and models: Global Biogeochemical Cycles, v. 23, no. GB2010, 14 p., doi:10.1029/2008GB003425.

Turnipseed, D.P., and Sauer, V.B., 2010, Discharge measurements at gaging stations: U.S. Geological Survey Techniques and Methods, book 3, chap. A8, 87 p. (Also available at http://pubs.usgs.gov/tm/tm3-a8/.)

U.S. Energy Information Administration, 2012, U.S. Energy Information Administration International Energy Statistics through 2010: U.S. Energy Information Administration web site, accessed October 26, 2012, at http://www.eia.gov/cfapps/ipdbproject/iedindex3.cfm?tid=1&pid=1&aid=2&cid=regions&syid=1980&eyid=2010&unit=TST.

U.S. Environmental Protection Agancy, 2002, Method 1631—Mercury in water by oxidation, purge and trap, and cold vapor atomic fluorescence spectrometry: U.S. Environmental Protection Agency, Revision E, EPA 821-R-95-027.

U.S. Fish and Wildlife Service, variously dated, National Wetlands Inventory, accessed September 10, 2012, at http://www.fws.gov/wetlands/Data/State-Downloads.html.

U.S. Geological Survey, variously dated, National field manual for the collection of water-quality data: U.S. Geological Survey Techniques of Water-Resources Investigations, book 9, chaps. A1–A9. (Also available at http://water.usgs.gov/owq/FieldManual/.)

Weishaar, J.L., Aiken, G.R., Bergamaschi, B.A., Fram, M.S., Fuji, R., and Mopper, K., 2003, Evaluation of specific ultraviolet absorbance as an indicator of the chemical composition and reactivity of dissolved organic carbon: Environmental Science and Technology, v. 37, p. 4,702–4,708.

Wiener, J.G., Krabbenhoft, D.P., Heinz, G.H., and Scheuhammer, A.M., 2003, Ecotoxicology of mercury, in Hoffman, D.J., Rattner, B.A., and Burton, G.A.J., eds., Handbook of Ecotoxicology: CRC Press, p. 1290.